CREDIT SCORE SECRETS

CREDIT SCORE SECRETS

Unlocking the Path to Financial Health

AUGUST RAINES

QuantumQuill Press

CONTENTS

CHAPTER 1

Introduction

The financial matrix known as the credit score was created by Fair Isaac in the 50s and first went into widespread use in 1989 as the FICO score. The original purpose was to help lenders make decisions about whom they would lend to and what interest rates they'd charge. Today, one's credit score is used for many more purposes. Many employers now pull your credit score as just one factor in screening for jobs. Mortgage lenders now assign higher interest rates to those with lower credit scores. How is all of this even legal? How is this process even remotely fair? If it's true that there are only three sentient beings in the universe who understand derivatives, how can literally hundreds of financial aspects of one's life be distilled down into a single number? This book will find these questions and many more surrounding your three-digit score.

No single consumer metric is more significant than the three-digit number that measures your creditworthiness. Your credit score not only tells potential lenders what kind of risk you are, but also gives employers, landlords, and insurance companies equal insights into your financial life. Everyone today is familiar with Where's Waldo? but a credit score performs the more important function of finding, understanding, and classifying you. Whether others can help you or, hands tied behind your back, harm your chances at improving your life largely hangs on this number. An improved understanding about what it is, goes into calculating it, how to nurture and protect it, and why you believe what you do about it remains the goal of this book.

CHAPTER 2

Understanding Credit Scores

The financial scoring model used today, the FICO score, is proprietary and is not shared either with the public or industry. Additionally, the scoring models used tend to change for the riskiest of borrowers but remain relatively stable once the individual falls into the remainder of the categories. Over the last 10 years, consumers have gained access to their credit reports and scores. Where should they look to uncover the information they will need about how to calculate their score? To start, view is to go online to any number of websites and request a copy of your report. However, this information tends to confound you rather than point you in a specific direction. A beneficial approach is to go to the methodology behind the score calculation and look to understand how that model affects scores.

Financial literacy has been described as a continuum leading from no knowledge to an expert level with a high degree of competency. When it comes to credit literacy, a level of very high competency is required to understand how credit scores are developed, calculated, and the overall impact of scores on the individual. Negative events surrounding the use of credit (debt) have increased in everyday headlines: downsizing, layoffs, bankruptcies, repossessions, and evictions. These events are curbing our national appetite to leverage ourselves further and deeper. Yet we face the largest mortgage debt, and personal debt obligations have snowballed. The smartest goal people can make for personal and family finances is to discover how credit works and how to fix those issues that relate to our credit.

CHAPTER 3

Factors Affecting Your Credit Score

...As we all know, having a lot of debt can be a heavy burden and create stress and anxiety around the home. High amounts of debt can mean that a person continuously delays on bills and payments. We all know that having debt is something that is important when trying to improve your credit score. The next time you go to a bank to ask for a loan or use a credit card, your creditor will look at your minimum payment that is shown on your credit reports. You are more likely to qualify for a larger loan when you have lower debt with an established history of paying off your accounts. This is why when you apply for a mortgage, for example, there is a benchmark that must be met in order to qualify. These are things to consider about what impacts your credit score and what you can do to improve your score. It is good to have an experienced credit repair professional guiding you through qualitative steps that have the biggest impact.

Remember, all your payments must be on time, not only to this ...

Late payments and debt are the largest factors affecting your credit score. Therefore, it is important that you stay current with all of your payments. Pay at least the minimum amount due and talk to your lenders or creditors to see if you will qualify for a modified payment plan or for any other customer relief programs. In some cases, the lenders do have programs that allow for a pause of payment without hurting your credit. However, make sure you call your lender to stop payments. Additionally, if you need help with managing your money and finances, you may want to hire a credit repair professional who can speak with many of your current and previous creditors to arrange for new payment arrangements. Other payment arrangements might include deferment of payments or settlement for a lower amount on what is owed. All of these actions will help you manage your debt and keep your payments current. Keep in mind that you must immediately stop using any credit card once you call the creditor to cancel the payment.

CHAPTER 4

Improving Your Credit Score

Be aware that there are no quick fixes. Set realistic expectations regarding credit improvement. Typically, most people need at least 9-12 months to see significant improvement in their score. Building a good credit report is a matter of trying to keep a low overall debt, mixing the types of credit that you have, establishing a long credit history, and helping others by being an authorized user on their accounts.

When trying to establish or rebuild credit, or when trying to get a large amount of credit such as a mortgage, there are a few actions that need extra attention and care. This includes making sure all payments are on time, ensuring that your credit report is accurate, minimizing the number of credit inquiries (checks into your credit by someone who is considering lending you money), and lowering your outstanding credit card debt. Making these alterations can lead to improvements in your credit score over time.

Despite popular opinion, running your credit report once a year through AnnualCreditReport.com does not hurt your score, nor does having a lender pull your credit score. Checking to see if a company pulled your credit score also does not lower your score.

- Increase your lines of credit. Pay on time and if you can't pay the full balance, pay more than the minimum due. Also, having a mix of revolving credit and installment loans can help. Too much credit can be a negative, but by adding a credit card or small loan to your credit mix and using it wisely, you can improve your credit score.

- Keep unused credit cards open so that your utilization rate decreases. The older your credit history, the better your score. It takes time to establish a positive track record.

- Review your credit report regularly. Make sure everything is accurate. You're entitled to one free credit report each year from each of the three major credit bureaus (Equifax, Experian, and TransUnion). You can request your free report by visiting AnnualCreditReporting.com.

Focusing on positive credit-building habits can significantly improve one's credit score. These are some simple ways to maintain a healthy score:

CHAPTER 5

Managing Credit Card Debt

A new credit card may be a godsend if you utilize it to transfer high-interest balances onto a credit card that offers a low or zero interest introductory period. Some card issuers even allow you to move the debt from other types of accounts, such as personal loans. Just remember that these offers usually have expiration dates, meaning zero interest may eventually become hovering interest. The good news, though, is that if you do the arithmetic, you may have some useful moves to make as the introductory period nears its end. Another piece of good news: Even just "shopping" for a balance transfer won't affect your credit score. Card offerings are considered a soft credit pull and do not make an impact, aside from the 3% of the debt they save you. And only then if that's the right number for you.

"Start working on paying down your credit cards" is something you see written a lot in these kinds of articles, and this one is no exception. Credit cards come with high interest rates, often as high as 25% or more, and the money you give the bank in interest is money you can't save or invest in the future. But even before you put the brakes on other spending, look into transferring the balances from high-interest cards to those with lower annual rates. Even if it costs you 3% of the amount being transferred, you may be better off paying that fee in a one-time transaction than the ongoing high interest rate. Although you have to be in good standing with the card issuer, meaning you must be up to date on your payments, you can usually transfer a balance up to your new card's credit limit. It's like the opening of a gate, letting you into a field of lower interest payments.

CHAPTER 6

Paying Off Loans and Debts

Or, with less than 15% of your net monthly income in long-term debt payments, an applicant will go through all the health tests. From 16% to 30%, the score will be penalized in the risk ratio. From 31% to 40% of income, the risk-reward coefficient may reach up to 2.5 times the risk rate. This happens both in concession franchises from franchises that offer up to 100% financing and attracts many borrowers. With these percentages, they are classified as conservative lending. A great visionary has succeeded in moderately rising to 2.5% of this rate, healthed within a prudent.

In a loan with a longer term, the margin for some mishap along the way is greater. Statistically, the probability of being late also comes with the score in the account, whether you like it or not. Your score is harmed when the capital amount of the installments is reduced quickly. If this happens regularly, it may be a sign that your financial health is no longer so good. A residual debt is an indication of the degree to which your income can pay off existing long-term debt. Low percentages give banks the security that you can afford your proposed loan. The margin left in your income will trigger the risk reward, or in other words, the correction factor that every financial institution applies to a customer in order not to run out very soon if you are late with the accounts or even more, break the relationship. This percentage works as a multiplication factor.

Myth says that canceling a great loan, like a mortgage, slows down your credit score. Also, maintaining a low residual debt is the way to keep it up. Understand! How can a mortgage, for example, pull your score down if you keep paying it on time?

CHAPTER 7

Building a Positive Credit History

What, however, is credit history? The credit bureaus, or credit reporting companies, are compilations of data regarding the management of financial records. This history often encompasses ten years of past borrowing in six-month increments. It is with these "records" that may include the number and type of accounts held, status of said accounts, and proper, 1G Utilizing Unsecured Credit cards varied payment activity along with the length of time that this activity has been maintained. Examples of negative credit, unfortunately, include filing for bankruptcy and taking on collections. Efforts to form a strong moral discipline during the capture this favorable record are only possible through repeated attempts. Furthermore, it promotes knowledge in combination with good habits, which indicates the level of intelligence possessed. If an individual can utilize either an unsecured credit card or a loan, these endeavors suggest that the borrower is likely a successful individual who has several good qualities. Profiles can also find out if an individual has been employed within the same job and if the individual has held any established checking and savings accounts over a period, of those options.

Let's say your parents have always rented. You're raised to never borrow. On the other hand, let's say your parents always owned a home and you've had an education beyond a bachelor's degree. Statistically speaking, you're predicted to have a high FICO credit score. They don't intend for you to take it as a stigma, but given America's financial literacy rate today, the fact that FICO scores include the study of credit history doesn't qualify everyone to carry a respectable score. When you open and maintain an account with a creditor who agrees to report items to the credit bureaus – Equifax, Experian, and TransUnion – positive entries help to support a good credit history. However, reflecting back on the results of a national survey of 3,151 participants revealed little understanding of the average American adult's capability in terms of maintaining a solid credit history.

CHAPTER 8

Avoiding Credit Score Mistakes

The first thing to remember is basics of a credit score. The whole idea for improving a credit score is to present a financial lifestyle that shows the capacity to sustain debt plus the responsible management of said obligations. Consequently, borrowing too much money and, even worse, non-payment of bills, will eventually indicate that the credit problems that you are experiencing are causing you great difficulties and are manageable. This is clearly reflected in your credit reports and almost inevitably causing your credit score to drop. Due to the availability of credit under the credit reporting system, a positive behavior will eventually cost you a raised credit score. If you are late with payments or are flooded with debts, then you are sending the wrong message. Simply put, it seems that you may not realize the potential effect on your credit score when you make the decision to prioritize another debt.

Even if you have been following all the right steps and advice, it is still possible to make serious mistakes that can postpone or derail your repairs to your credit score. Using violative tricks, regardless of how exciting they can be or even if they work in obtaining credit you are not financially capable to acquire, can only lead to further complications. Just think of these the next time that you are tempted to make a move that is too good to be true and is not acceptable. Adhering to the following rules can help you avoid these mistakes, make important progress in repairing your credit score, and improve your capacity to borrow funds and to be capable of qualifying for loans.

Monitoring Your Credit Score

Also, most banks and credit card companies now offer their own credit score tracking services. Often they are tied to a credit monitoring feature which will also alert you to potential fraud on your accounts. These sites may also offer myriad advice for how to lift your credit score, such as paying down a certain specific loan that is being held against you or selling off a high-balance credit card. Finally, certain union websites may offer free or steeply discounted credit monitoring services as well. It is always worth a Google just to check!

You can keep yourself on track regarding the health of your credit score in a number of ways. Since, as we have discussed, it is the number one driving factor in your access to loans and the interest rates you will be given – and since even the minor differences in interest rate can save you tens of thousands of dollars on loans over the course of your lifetime – it can be well worthwhile to monitor your credit score carefully. A number of websites offer a free monitoring service where they update your credit score every month. The peculiar bonus to this service is that once you are receiving regular updates on your credit score, you can opt to be notified when your credit score changes. If this happens unexpectedly, it can be a sign of fraud or identity theft, allowing you to get back on the path to resolution as soon as possible.

CHAPTER 10

Credit Score Myths Debunked

1. Your income is included in your credit score. Many people are shocked to learn that the credit scoring system does not count or consider their current income. Whether you make $20,000 or $200,000 makes absolutely no difference! Employment information and almost any personal information about someone – their age, race, marital status, income, assets, or employment – cannot be used to determine their credit score. After all, credit scores are only intended to be a measure of the risk of not paying a debt as agreed, not a measure of how much money you have. The only income-related consideration when applying for a loan is whether your income is enough to support the new credit payments. Assumptions about income may be made based on the job history, but a credit score is blind about your income and employment. Today, many financial scams specifically target people who believe that money is the key to a high credit score; many individuals are willing to pay a substantial upfront fee for instant expert advice. Prevent blowback from this misconception through knowledge and persistence. Randomly paying for advice without investigating the foundation of your belief is a recipe for disaster.

Credit Score Secrets: Unlocking the Path to Financial Health uncovered over 50 credit score myths that many people believe. The myths reflected a wide range of common misperceptions about credit scores and the credit scoring process, but the good news is that clearing up the myths is easy! These 10 common myths and misconceptions hold people back and reinforce negative credit score behaviors. By understanding the truth, you will be able to improve your credit score and never make these mistakes again.

CHAPTER 11

The Impact of Credit Scores on Financial Health

Moreover, many businesses use credit scores and credit reports in their respective processes. For instance, insurance companies use credit scores in their pricing for particular product offerings, where allowed. The use of credit scores in insurance is coined insurance credit scores. Additionally, cable and cell phone companies use credit scores and credit reports for deposits or deposit waivers for equipment rental or setup fees, and the hiring process of potential employees, among other corporate purposes.

Many people see credit scores merely as a summary of a consumer's financial responsibility, and indeed this is one small piece of the overall puzzle. Consumers and small businesses with higher credit scores generally receive lower-priced credit overall in the form of mortgages, personal loans, car loans, and credit cards, while those with lower credit scores generally receive higher-priced credit or are unable to obtain credit altogether. Therefore, one of the biggest challenges with a low credit score or bad credit is a consumer's reduced access to credit and influence over the terms of that credit, which can prevent consumers from achieving their personal or financial goals or managing other life events, for instance, emergencies and other life changes. In some cases, consumers may resort to nontraditional forms of credit or informal lending structures with higher costs of credit when traditional credit is not available to them. Credit scores and reports can thus play a significant role in a consumer's or a small business owner's financial life.

CHAPTER 12

Credit Score and Loan Applications

When a credit report is first generated and analyzed from an examination of past experiences with debt, it should be evidence of an ability and willingness to repay. Both the lender and the consumer alike are more likely to perceive this as a favorable characteristic. The marketplace has built a strong connection between a credit report and a willingness as well as an ability to satisfy future debt obligations, and some have even likened the report to a crystal ball. Unfortunately, with no quantitative data, the banker's crystal ball is nothing more than a Magic Eight Ball. However, if the glimmer that the personal characteristics shown in the report and interpreted correctly, such as integrity, perseverance, resourcefulness, and teamwork, is holding this prism to the light, the answer falls forth from MAXIMA – affirmative! The scores created by the Credit Report Act ultimately generate strong feelings in people. A certain number on a report not only has the capability to allow Americans to fulfill major housing-related goals but also represents standing in the community. The idea that this number could render someone indispensable goes back centuries. In Shakespeare's time, it was the number of an account, not a credit score, that made the difference!

When consumers complete a formal loan application, two credit score-related notices apply. The first is a description of their rights under the Equal Credit Opportunity Act. If they are denied, it provides the basis for the actions the creditor has taken. The second is a disclosure with the numerical credit score that the lender used in processing their application. This section takes a look at each notice.

CHAPTER 13

Credit Score and Mortgage Approval

Could you guess what fresh, juicy apple strudel and a mortgage approval have in common? We'll give you a hint. It's not the kitchen! They are both the products of various preparation steps. From kitchen countertops and mortgage pre-approvals, the experience readies all of us for that well-planned, approachable conversation. Do you see how these scenarios reveal so much about smooth preparation? Finely sliced apples. A crease-resistant pastry garnished with powdered sugar. Who wouldn't admire that? Try walking into a bank to begin a conversation about becoming an important local homeowner without a long-toothed credit file stronger in chin like a long-toothed deer. We couldn't have obtained a mortgage pre-approval or apple strudel without preparation planning. Now that the mortgage's approval dictates your credit file knows better, go back to kitchen drums! It's time to bake, cook, and crack open your first borrowing chapter.

Lenders can't predict the future. The presence of negative credit items is a clue, but it isn't fate. Understanding and taking steps before applying often tune credit files, including those with negative credit items, from auto-denial to "approve." Ever walk through a shopping mall when all is quiet? It's a different walk than when crowds are present. Conversations buzz alive when people accompany you. When alone, only your thoughts fill the air (when you breathe through your mask). Credit files are like that too. A credit file often looks out of balance, incomplete, or neglectful. Negative comments, combined with a low credit score, paint a doomsday picture. You become unapproachable. Conversations falter, though your purpose is keen and serious. Tumbleweeds scratch at the mind. Prepare early and walk confidently. The mortgage loan is your companion, your passport to homeownership and its treasured conversations.

CHAPTER 14

Credit Score and Auto Loans

This is one popular way for the poor credit consumer to build their credit. They can go to the bigger used car dealers that also make loans and require proof of a steady job while this is important. There are national companies that make car loans to consumers, regardless of their credit status, and will report the loan payment to the credit bureaus. The best part is that a consumer can get a loan with just a pay stub to prove that he can pay the loan. A steady job is the key. However, this process is the least known, but very important for those who need some kind of auto transportation.

Just because you have a low or not so perfect credit score does not mean you can't get an auto loan. The problem is that financing a vehicle can be really expensive for someone with poor credit. Finance charges can be close to, in some cases, twice as much as a person who has excellent credit. This is an example of how credit can be very costly to someone who has neglected their credit history. So, here it comes, here is my score of the poor consumer who can't buy a car and will travel on public transportation or will resort to part-time car rental if they need to travel anywhere.

CHAPTER 15

Credit Score and Credit Card Applications

A new card application doesn't just affect your credit score. A CRA is not required by law to even include inquiries or credit reports within the past 12 months in credit scores. Because of your credit score, you're really only on the hook here for over two years. Of course submitting to more APRs due to lower credit scores and increased pending use can hurt, but like other negative written criteria, 15% of the help cards have a good rating. When you can, avoid buying a card unless you have a clear vision of the product you want and you are confident that you can be granted and continue to be considered psychologically. Do not risk the quality of your credit score to save 10% at the particular department store where creditors like it or to get this annuity discount. Optimal decisions for the current financial debt. Create a list. If you want to have a good credit score and improve your financial life, you just need to take a few critical steps towards this goal.

There are many factors that determine your credit score - drivers recorded on the databases kept by the major CRAs, including Experian, TransUnion, and Equifax. More people have? He or she does. But most formulations are based on this type of credit score. These applications can make up to 10% of the total credit score, depending on how many times you've creditors been to the car dealership or home shopping center and "overlooked" before you have paid it or been knocking on their front door too much. Learn more about the following credit information sections? And impact your credit score and what not to do.

Credit Score and Insurance Premiums

Here's the dirty little secret: your credit score can and does affect the premiums you may have to pay. Low scores can be indicative of increased credit risk. Accordingly, insurance companies may have a belief, substantiated or not, that those with lower scores have a higher "insured risk" incidence. Intuitively, this doesn't sound too far off base. People with poor credit may be desperate, may be more prone to settle quickly with a property damage claim, while those with solid credit put up a bigger fight. Courts have ruled in favor of insurance companies, stipulating that there's a statistically significant relationship between scores and claim representation, with claim-to-reserve ratios revealing that policyholders with higher "financial responsibility" have lower costs per claim.

While there's no official report to consult, clinical deciphering of insurance company practices makes it clear that credit scores impact homeowners (residence), auto and other property and casualty insurance rates. By now we're familiar with the notion of "good driver" rates: if you've had no at-fault accidents (usually for a three-year period) and no moving traffic violations, you qualify for a discount from both the driving record and credit rating credits. It's hard to get an insurance policy (or at least a good one) if your credit is limited or completely missing. This chapter takes a look at the credit-casualty connection.

CHAPTER 17

Credit Score and Employment Opportunities

The use of credit scores by employers varies. Thirty-one percent of employers report using credit checks to screen applicants in a 2010 survey conducted by the Society for Human Resource Management (SHRM), up from 18% in 2006. Small employers are less likely to use credit checks on job applicants than large employers overall, 35% of employers with 5,000 to 10,000 employees participated in 2010, dwarfing the 15% of employers with fewer than 100 employees that reported using credit checks. Previous research documents that employers view a poor credit score as an indicator of an applicant who is less likely to handle job responsibilities—particularly financial or sensitive job functions—the adverse impact of the concomitant past financial issues on hiring decisions tends to have a disproportionate impact on African American applicants. In particular, one study estimates that the increase in the unemployment rate resulted in a 6.5% reduction in the employment of African Americans compared with a 5.1% reduction in the employment of European Americans in occupations with high rates of credit check usage. Moreover, employers are less likely to extend. Empirical evidence also suggests that employers who make use of credit reports are less likely to hire people who are working to improve their credit.

In addition to their application in credit screening, credit scores are used increasingly by employers as part of a broader background screening program. While employers do not have direct access to credit scores, they often receive modified versions of the risk scores sold to lending institutions for a variety of job classes. It has decried employment use of credit scores, arguing that they are not a valid indicator of trustworthiness or ability to perform a job, and therefore should not be used to screen job applicants. Opponents also fear that credit score use will stigmatize individuals who are unable to repay their debts. In contrast, supporters argue that credit scores are highly predictive of behavior in other walks of life and can be used to better predict performance and trustworthiness than other records that are available. Employers emphasize that credit scores are not used as the sole factor in making hiring decisions. Extensive background checks, tests, references, etc., are used in conjunction with credit scores.

CHAPTER 18

Credit Score and Rental Applications

It's important for a screening model to calculate your score based more heavily on payment history than your length of credit history, since it helps landlords to be confident that you won't be practicing your rock band until the early hours and disturbing other tenants. Applicants may also be deemed as risky if the credit report contains unresolved balances or accounts in collection, so ensuring the amount owed is current is key to being granted a lease. You can find the same information as the landlord screening model on the TransUnion and Equifax credit reports that you receive at no charge. These reports also allow you to see how you look in the other major scoring models, which provide scores in a range that is similar to the FICO range (300 to 850), and usually factors things like payment history, amounts owed, age of credit history, new credit inquiries, and types of credit into the score calculations.

When you apply for an apartment or a house, the landlord or property management company may check your credit as part of running a background check. This is a common, legal practice and helps protect landlords from renting to someone with a poor payment history or a tendency to break rental agreements. But here's a surprise - the landlord generally does not see your actual credit report. Instead, they see a customized credit score that is formulated specifically for rental decisions known as an "applicant scoring model." You can think of it as a customized flavor of the main credit scoring models called scoring algorithms. The tenant screening scoring algorithm is designed to look at indicators such as late payments or outstanding balances that are indicative of a rental guarantee risk, versus the likelihood that the applicant will be a good tenant.

CHAPTER 19

Credit Score and Utility Services

The advance deposit prevents the customer from accumulating a large bill before the utility company can recoup its costs through the deposit, which reduces the risk that the utility recognizes for the operation of the customer. When the utility company refunds the deposit, the customers may find it more difficult to make the payment, which also increases the risk. Many customers who receive free service, such as phone lines, refuse to pay their accumulated bills, resulting in missed deposits. This occurs when a stood or terminated account is related to a tenant and not the owner of the individual address rental property, or if the mistaken association is reported. Therefore, the result of the incorrect association is that the tenure owner is refused service.

When the operating company charges a high deposit for utility, for instance after the credit report, there are invalid items and often utility companies will correct or redirect the errors which are removed from the account or will not require the payment of the advance deposit. A second utility security deposit for a particular customer has occurred between the date of the deposit for a sixty-eight day time deposit. If the credit report has a particular form of bankruptcy, the utility company will perform that deposit.

Credit scores are an important factor when citizens are applying for utility service. For people with a thin credit file, paying higher deposits for utility services damages the credit, leading to costlier credit and less access to credit from traditional financial institutions. We should strive to ensure that people have access to low-cost credit, especially people who are on low incomes.

CHAPTER 20

Credit Score and Interest Rates

Final loan approval is often conditional on a number of factors, but a specific waiting period may denote the earliest day a mortgage can close. The closing date is further affected by the finance condition, which is a way to get the flexibility needed, for instance, should the rate lock expire before closing. Making sure that you have this vital piece of paper before waiting for a mortgage loan approval is an important personal credit management task. An eligible collateral installment loan is an installment loan with a lower interest rate than credit card balances. Some examples of this include auto loans, student loans, and unless managed properly, new furniture and appliances. If demonstrating portfolio diversity is an issue, the existence of various types of collateral loans in the file can be a positive in your score.

Since most people don't have credit scores above 800, they generally won't qualify for the best rates. Knowing that some people will have a tough time bringing their scores up to 800 and beyond, the credit scoring powers that be still want these consumers to have a goal and put incentives in place in the form of rate reciprocity. In other words, the better your credit score is, the lower interest rate you can expect to receive on a loan. Conversely, as your credit score drops, your interest rate rises, and they rise significantly. The increase in the monthly payment on a 30-year fixed-rate mortgage, which is the most significant loan in most people's lives, due to an increase in the rate you receive is exponential as your credit score drops. At these escalated rates, the full repayment of a 30-year fixed-rate mortgage many times over can occur just by nudging the rate upward a little, but as a result of what appears to be just a somewhat decreasing credit score.

CHAPTER 21

Credit Score and Financial Planning

Chapter 6 applied science to reveal your credit habits; Chapter 7 introduced a model to moderate one element of financial risk. Manipulating the risk and risk factors of Chapters 1 and 2 is, over time, the pathology resulting in the national norm of first-dollar-paying versus a health saving behavior. The norm is that a small sum, not $1, $8,000 per year set aside is the solution to the credit problem discovered in the foregoing chapter. We need another tool. Could you use more money in your pockets, money reflected in better interest rates, on a car loan, and house loan, with insurance and maintenance outlays better controlled alongside everyday auto costs? Some employers offer benefits contributing to a significant lifestyle change. Over time, a health savings account could be a force contributing to that desired shift in car expense. With vision and attention, a health savings account may solve a lot more than health expenses. It guides your financial future. It also improves mandatory spending, which enhances one of two credit elements, payment history, and credit availability.

Have you disabused the notion that checking your score negatively affects it? Are your finances and credit everything you would hope? Have you developed goals you will not reach attractive to you? A motivational approach to credit results in strategic planning based on the specific goal in mind – a goal to reach a credit score of 760 or above. "How," you might ask, "is aiming high satisfying?" Remember the best characteristic of the credit system? It is relatively easy to control. If you want a 760+, adopt habits consistent with the goal, and you will get there. We begin the next section addressing some of the more jaded myths driving our financial lives.

CHAPTER 22

Credit Score and Retirement Planning

It is a little known fact, but credit does play a significant role in our retirement. It is important no matter what financial stage you are in. First, you cannot retire early and travel the world as planned if your credit score is not good since you will also have a difficult time paying those dream bills. Your credit history can even affect your ability to get retirement communities or senior housing and even affect other decisions. Secondly, there is a temptation to take a loan against the retirement fund or pay off your credit. This is not recommended unless it is your only solution. Taking a loan from your 401(k) can take a serious toll on your retirement fund and could force you to work longer than anticipated. Less money means that you will not have enough funds to invest and grow. Therefore, assess your current financial situation and make a clear retirement plan before you make the decision to withdraw funds from your retirement account, especially any pre-tax retirement account. A bad credit can increase the rate you will be charged.

To most people, retirement seems like a long way away. Experts tell them that they have to start planning now, but retirement is an abstract plan that matures decades down the road. In this context, it may be difficult to see how a good credit score relates to retirement plans. However, it is important to stress that a good credit history can make for great retirement planning. Poor credit can mar those golden years. Indeed, many experts say that your credit should be a major focus when it comes to planning for your retirement. Take control of your credit and the path to retirement-planning success will be made that much smoother.

CHAPTER 23

Credit Score and Debt Consolidation

In this paper, we provide some new evidence on the complementary relationship between traditional banking and financial technology (fintech) credit markets based on the specific major product of debt consolidation lending in the United States. The conceptual foundation of our hypothesis is that lenders offered by fintech platforms may actively pursue more informed and less-informed consumers in order to maximize their expected profits and maximize the volume of approved applications; maximize profits by strategically competing with the traditional bank lenders, matching their debt consolidation offerings; and target financially vulnerable consumers.

Once credit expectations stabilize, matched lenders resume approving consolidating loans with attractive features. Given these credit loss incentives, some matched lenders will tend to approve borrowers who indicate some level of awareness of and concern about the hazards of long-term over-indebtedness, but others will instead (a) target the more vulnerable borrowers and/or (b) be more amenable than bank lenders to financing risky debt consolidation plans. Using consumer credit panel data coupled with detailed administrative data on credit inquiries over 2013-2016, we find robust evidence of the latter pattern. The matched lenders respond to the availability of credit information held by traditional banks by approving riskier debt consolidation loans.

Debt consolidation is the process of combining multiple debts into a single, new, larger loan that will usually have a lower interest rate. This makes payment more convenient and easier. Monthly savings are created because, with a lower interest rate, the same amount of monthly payments goes toward paying the loan principal, reducing it more quickly. Because the principal decreases more quickly, the interest paid over the life of the loan is less. The consolidation loan typically has a longer term, translating into lower monthly payments. Debt consolidation can also lead to an increase in credit score. Combined stated that lower interest rates and a reduction in loan balances will typically be observed in around 2-3 months after loan closing. Debt consolidation is available to most consumers, excluding those with the worst credit scores.

CHAPTER 24

Credit Score and Identity Theft

A credit score literally changes on a daily basis. Paying down credit card balances or having an increase in a credit line can affect a credit score and may be viewed by a credit report company. Because of the frequent changes in a credit score, credit score repair is considered a moving target and may take time. A good credit score can be obtained from hard work, a good plan, and will keep credit score goals and dreams on track. To protect your identity, consider exponential and technology risk analysis, ongoing monitoring, and items that are not on the credit reporting file.

Credit scores are more important than ever before, yet many people don't understand how they are affected, how they are calculated, and how to use and protect their credit score. In 2017, there were 16.7 million Americans affected by identity theft. Between 2007 and 2017, approximately 160 million Americans have been affected by identity theft. Any methodology to handle your finances should include ways to handle your credit score. A good credit score helps with lower insurance rates, lower interest rates, and even lower deposits for utilities and cell phone contracts. A poor credit score can financially cause higher payments and deposits. Monitoring credit reports, identifying simple credit mistakes, and a good credit score can help secure financial health through better interest rates and less financial costs.

CHAPTER 25

Credit Score and Bankruptcy

Filing for bankruptcy can temporarily lower your FICO score, but you can rebuild your credit. At the same time, other negative data, such as judgments, foreclosures, liens, and other public records, can have a significant effect. Be aware that your FICO score takes all of these data points into account when it comes to your score. Bankruptcy is frequently an effective way to deal with serious financial problems. Chapter 7 and Chapter 13 bankruptcy are legal actions that give consumers who are struggling with overwhelming debt a way to eliminate or restructure their debt and get a financial fresh start. It's important to realize that certain debts cannot be discharged in a chapter 7 bankruptcy or in the majority of cases in chapter 13. Non-dischargeable debts include child support, most tax debts, most student loan debts, and amounts incurred through fraud or misrepresentation.

I have filed for bankruptcy. Can I ever get a good credit score? Bankruptcy alone won't prevent someone from having a good FICO score. Just as with every other aspect of getting your finances on track, the key is to make good financial choices afterwards. Bankruptcy and the time leading up to bankruptcy will lower your credit score, but you must understand that if you are filing for bankruptcy, your rating is likely to be low to begin with. You probably will have some type of court judgment listed, and possibly one or more charge-offs. After seven to 10 years, these negative entries will be purged from your file. Improving the rating of someone who recently filed is less about correcting data and more about making sound financial choices. As you start to build a positive history, the large bankruptcy will become less relevant, just as a series of delinquencies or a large debt balance becomes less relevant over time.

CHAPTER 26

Credit Score and Divorce

Itemizing debts and assets When you are in the process of getting a divorce, your first objective is to begin by listing around your household assets and debts. You should utilize the old approach of dividing and conquer. The idea here is for one spouse or partner to make a list of all the income, outgoings, and expenses of the household, while the other spouse or partner makes a list, captured all the liabilities and assets of the household. This will prove to be invaluable because if there is a disagreement or any kind of dispute, you need to back appealed to the listing. Consider carefully debts on credit reports in. Whether or not you were worried about the word comes in and the lawyers negotiate to carry out the best possible solution, it is essential for you to consider the word comes to your credit report. Anything until whether or not your divorce is finalized and whether or not your decree is accurate enough that has our details on it, both credit reports will still markings of us as reports from anywhere.

It is not uncommon for couples who are going through the process of getting a divorce to have financial issues. For example, it is not uncommon for financial issues to be identified as the third leading cause of divorce in the U.S. In today's tough times, financial problems can cause a lot of stress on any relationship. It has also become common for one or both parties going through the process of getting a divorce to have a low credit score. This article is designed to provide key information and key tips on anything and what you need to do to succeed in getting this number improved, in line with increased credit scores. Let's go ahead and start by stating anything and let my guest clothes were not affected, in terms of any negative information found on your credit report.

CHAPTER 27

Credit Score and Student Loans

Can I borrow as much student loan now as I need to and not risk my credit scores I might need to buy a home later? If you need to finance a home down the road, you will need good credit. Many lending institutions require at least three accounts which totaled together must not be more than 40% of your income, military guidelines are 45%, some lenders set this threshold as low as 35% of your income. Even if you find a mortgage company will give you a great rate with four brake lights - student loan accounts on your credit score, be aware there may be further student loan Poole in the form of lender guidelines. When you inquire about this, ask an underwriter - the person who ultimately must make a decision to fund or not fund - "How long do you require someone to demonstrate they have learned to manage income responsibly?" Equifax.com and TrueCredit.com recognize this problem, and have extended early alerts services to all consumers. Customers learn of new information such as late payments and lower credit scores that may happen due to student loans.

To add to the potential problem, companies that specialize in aiding students secure loans appropriately advertise such services to the world. That is, they offer student loans to a group of people; students about to head off to college. In today's world, they often do it on the web. When doing so also leaves a so-called inquiry that you applied for credit; and people - from credit bureaus to business consultants - who later view your credit report may not be able to tell that you are using a student loan to help make a dream come true.

It is very easy to destroy a credit score. But doing the opposite, boosting your credit score, takes time. Hopefully, the various inquiries about student loans you may receive will not only help you secure needed funds but also bring down your credit score. You need intermediating credit, such as paying the bills for the student loans as agreed. Use a student loan to take a number of steps forward, not a leap back.

CHAPTER 28

Credit Score and Small Business Loans

In this chapter and its corresponding appendices, I'll discuss mistakes that business owners and entrepreneurs make that negatively affect their credit scores. I'll also tell you why some of the usual strategies for improving your credit score might not be particularly effective in the eyes of many small business lenders and can even backfire—ultimately lowering your scores. Finally, I'll also give you tips for working with your existing suppliers and other vendors to build a positive business credit history.

But your personal credit score is another matter. It's the first place most lenders turn now when they are evaluating risk. In fact, in a survey compiled by the small business lending company LendingExpress and the research firm QJR Consulting, more than 75% of small businesses reported that it was harder to get a loan now than it was two years ago. Not surprisingly, the number-one reason these small business owners cited for rejection was their personal credit scores.

When you're first starting a business or seeking financing or credit to help it grow, your personal credit score will be one of the most important factors in any lender's evaluation of your small business loan application. You may be able to get a small business lender to look past your limited business credit history, lack of equipment, or other factors.

Lenders may even be willing to overlook things like high debt-to-income ratios or a new business that isn't profitable yet.

CHAPTER 29

Credit Score and International Credit

You will appear as a responsible borrower if you make your payments on time and in full under each of the terms set for a variety of loans. As well, you have the ability to repay your debts in full monthly without feeling any discomfort. You will demonstrate that you have maintained your credit history by the way you present it. Your report should show the credit accounts you have held open and in good standing during the last ten years. Periodically shop and apply for different types of credit, so that your reports can be examined with a variety of accounts - including, but not limited to, a car loan, excerpts, Visa and MasterCard, and perhaps one or two retail accounts, each reporting each month to their respective bureaus. You have consistently made your loan payments on time and your car loan contains a good mixture of numbers that have been made for a period of six months. You are timely with online rent payments. Even though they are six months old, they see you have the capacity to make a respectable payment for the first six months of payments according to the car loan terms. Data can be obtained from three or more banks, their online banking data and their credit card transactions for these accounts.

People have transacted business across international borders for centuries. However, when you first move to another country, your credit score will not move with you. There is no question that the process of establishing your credit history in a new country will be challenging and frustrating. You may be required to use only cash for a very long time. The way you present yourself when presenting your credit report to a prospective creditor will have an enormous impact on the decision to lend. The credit history you spent years building is suddenly not available for them to access. We will show you what is expected from you to attempt to secure a loan with these two huge negatives in our Credit Chapter.

CHAPTER 30

Credit Score and Credit Counseling

A firm that negotiates changes in the terms of your credit agreement with your creditors changes information currently reported on your credit record. This is true for revolving, installment, student, or mortgage loans. When a former or current creditor negotiates, you should present proof to the credit reporting agency that the creditor has agreed to recognize new terms. This verification is vital so that the credit reporting agencies update the file information correctly. If the correction is not made, just as when a creditor sells your information to a debt collector, be persistent in demanding the change be made. Since a statute of limitations sets up when negative information is reported, after that time has elapsed, the credit reporting agency must delete the file. Under no circumstance should any information be indicating the account is still open and unresolved be reported as "deleted settled for less than the full amount". Revolving accounts showing a balance owed when you apply for new loans can lower your credit score regardless of whether the account shows late payments.

The debt counseling matter: So, you find yourself in financial trouble. Making even the minimum payments on your debts is a struggle. You're receiving disturbing phone calls from collection agencies, or you are spending sleepless nights worried about where to get more money to pay your debts. If your financial situation becomes severe enough, you may want to consider engaging a credit counseling firm. Some reputable credit counseling firms provide valuable financial counseling, help you organize an orderly way to repay your bills, and help you achieve financial stability. How does engaging a consumer credit counseling firm influence your credit? That depends on how the firm deals with your creditors and if the firm can negotiate lower interest rates, waive finance charges, and a substantial minimum payment. If the firm claims that your failure to make your debt payments has been cured due to your involvement with the company, your credit record will be affected. In Chapter 26, we discuss credit counseling firms and provide recommended consumer counseling firms in Appendix D.

CHAPTER 31

Credit Score and Financial Education

But is this financial education enough? Some of the recent culprits who have destroyed our American Dream with their outright greed have had a college education, yet who in their right mind would say they have a working intelligence of even an average person? There plain and simple has not been any financial responsibility or education at any level of our current society or class structure in this country. We have a whole generation now spent on credit cards, a credit card education allowing all wannabes a chance to own anything! ASAP. Today, with the move of the credit scoring system and the distribution of credit secure accounts, the distribution of ID Theft, I cannot stress enough the need for a thorough and colorful education for our current students as well as our working-class people. In fact, for everyone. The financial freedom for this country is standing on the edge of a chasm. With that in my humble opinion, unless this program has been developed at the early teaching age level up to graduation, ensuring every student leaves their education with a secured, intact, spotless credit score, then we should not abate a day without implementing it further. Because in its lack, there is only missing time.

There has been a move afoot to incorporate financial education into our schools' curriculums. Some schools have opened actual banks on their campuses run by their students. In doing so, the students are not only learning about the banking industry but are also ensuring the necessity of banking services and can partake of those services through the bank in which they are working. The school banks are open to all students, and the students working in the bank are also the board of directors that make any banking policies. This program seems to have been working quite well. I wholeheartedly support this curriculum in all schools, public and private, to ensure that all students receive these basic skills.

CHAPTER 32

Conclusion

Based on the many topics discussed in 32 chapters in this short book, there are several key items to help you realize as you read this final conclusion: many financial challenges, including those experienced as you attempt to achieve or build healthy credit, are the same from individual to individual. Most individuals do not win the financial lottery at birth, and while the family may wish you financial health and well-being, a healthy credit score is rarely provided by inheritance, will, or trust fund. Lower interest rates will be awarded based on higher credit scores. Requirements of individuals and families can be anticipated and then properly planned for in that event. Obtaining a high credit score and retaining it is a lot easier than attempting to build one from the ground up in as little as a few years.

We know that building credit is an important aspect of financial well-being that can help you attain your life goals and wish list desires. Although the journey to your credit destination should be personally tailored, it is paved with timeless, basic concepts similar to street signs. Start by constructing, then maintaining good credit habits while avoiding significant roadblocks along your route. You'll then be sure to reach your destination with credit in tow. As you journey on the road to your credit score needs, remember the helpful experiences and cautionary tales along the way, and let them help you tell the next leg of your story.